Susan Hawthorne is an award-winning writer of poetry, fiction and non-fiction. Her works include eight collections of poetry. Her collection *Cow* (2011) was shortlisted for the Kenneth Slessor Poetry prize in the NSW Premier's Literary Awards and was a Finalist in the Audre Lorde Lesbian Poetry Prize (USA). *Earth's Breath* (2009) was shortlisted for the Judith Wright Poetry Prize. Susan has been the recipient of international residencies in Turkey, Italy and India. She has translated literary works from Sanskrit, Greek and Latin and her books have been translated into German, Spanish, Arabic, French and Czech. She was the winner of the 2017 Penguin Random House Best Achievement in Writing in the Inspire Awards for her work increasing awareness about epilepsy and the politics of disability. In addition to her writing she has taught English to Arabic women, worked in Aboriginal education, in universities and been an aerialist in a circus.

Other books by Susan Hawthorne

poetry
Lupa and Lamb (2014)
Valence: Considering War through Poetry and Theory (2011, chapbook)
Cow (2011)
Earth's Breath (2009)
Unsettling the Land (with Suzanne Bellamy, 2008, chapbook)
The Butterfly Effect (2005)
Bird and Other Writings on Epilepsy (1999)
The Language in My Tongue (1993)

fiction
Dark Matters (2017)
Limen (2013, verse novel)
The Falling Woman (1992/2004)

non-fiction
Bibliodiversity: A Manifesto for Independent Publishing (2014)
Wild Politics: Feminism, Globalisation and Bio/diversity (2002)
The Spinifex Quiz Book (1993)

anthologies
Lesbian Poets and Writers: Live Encounters (2018)
Horse Dreams: The Meaning of Horses in Women's Lives (with Jan Fook and Renate Klein, 2004)
Cat Tales: The Meaning of Cats in Women's Lives (with Jan Fook and Renate Klein, 2003)
September 11, 2001: Feminist Perspectives (with Bronwyn Winter, 2002)
Cyberfeminism: Connectivity, Critique and Creativity (with Renate Klein, 1999)
Car Maintenance, Explosives and Love and Other Lesbian Writings (with Cathie Dunsford and Susan Sayer, 1997)
Australia for Women: Travel and Culture (with Renate Klein, 1994)
Angels of Power and Other Reproductive Creations (with Renate Klein, 1991)
The Exploding Frangipani: Lesbian Writing from Australia and New Zealand (with Cathie Dunsford, 1990)
Moments of Desire: Sex and Sensuality by Australian Feminist Writers (with Jenny Pausacker, 1989)
Difference: Writings by Women (1985)

The SACKING *of the* MUSES

SUSAN HAWTHORNE

SPINIFEX

First published by Spinifex Press, 2019

Spinifex Press Pty Ltd
PO Box 5270, North Geelong, VIC 3215, Australia
PO Box 105, Mission Beach, QLD 4852, Australia

women@spinifexpress.com.au
www.spinifexpress.com.au

Cover design by Deb Snibson, MAPG
Typesetting by Helen Christie, Blue Wren Books
Typeset in Athelas
Printed by McPherson's Printing Group

NATIONAL LIBRARY OF AUSTRALIA
A catalogue record for this book is available from the National Library of Australia

ISBN: 9781925950007 (paperback)
ISBN: 9781925950014 (ebook: epub)
ISBN: 9781925950021 (ebook: pdf)
ISBN: 9781925950038 (ebook: kindle)

Cover photo is of Kapila Venu performing the classical Indian theatre form Nangiar Koothu. This was a performance based on the story of Pūtanā.
Photo © Susan Hawthorne, 2009.

FSC www.fsc.org
MIX
Paper from responsible sources
FSC® C001695

Contents

Prologue

In 2009, I had the good fortune to have an Asialink Literature Residency in Chennai. About a week into my stay by circumstances that can only be called serendipitous I met Mangai, a feminist playwright, actor and director. Over the next months we collaborated on choreography of plays and on aerials workshops. One night, at Mangai's instigation, I found myself the pillion on a motorbike on my way to a performance of Nangiar Koothu by Kapila Venu. This extraordinary classical theatre form involves eye movements, particular movements of the limbs, body and head which transcend the need for verbal language. Out of that came my first poem in the sequence 'Temper of the Dance'. In the week following my first meeting with Mangai, I attended a performance of Bharatanatyam, another Tamil dance tradition. Among the performances was one based on the story of Ambā that Mangai directed. On subsequent evenings, the story of Draupadī, of Kṛṣṇa and others were performed. I could not have written these poems had I not met Mangai when I did.

I began learning Sanskrit in 2007 and have continued to do so. Every year brings more surprise poems based on my exposure to new stories from old texts. Or in the case of śleṣa (slesha) a different approach to writing poetry. Śleṣa has been called 'extreme poetry' because it enables the poet to express two different sentences with different meanings using what appear to be the same words. As a lesbian poet I find myself doing this, not through sentences but through codes. Some of these can be found in the third section. Śleṣa has also been called unnatural. Yigal Bronner in his book on śleṣa, *Extreme Poetry: The South Asian Movement of Simultaneous Narration*, notes that not only has it been called unnatural but also "an extravagant display that necessarily comes at the expense of plot and is therefore 'decadent', 'torturous', 'disgusting', and even 'indecent' and 'criminal'". You can see why I would be enticed by this poetic technique.

My journey into ancient languages was begun at age twelve, when I learnt Latin. But I was told to drop it after just two years. I picked it up again much later and well after I had studied Ancient Greek in the 1980s. One of the thrills of Greek is translating poems by Sappho.

The final sequence of poems in this book was written before, during and after the election of Donald Trump. The Muses of the ancient world have ideas and they consider how they might occupy contemporary cities, the art world and the world of politics to create change. They are the daughters of Mnemosyne—whose name is related to the word mnemonic—who is the Greek goddess of memory. She is invoked at the beginning of epic poems in order to help the poet recall the work accurately. Mnemosyne has a critical role to play in oral literature and she emerges again in feminist writing. In the early 1970s, I read Monique Wittig's *Les Guérillères*. She calls on her lesbian readers to remember a time when women were not slaves. In a modern invocation to Mnemosyne she wrote: "... remember. Make an effort to remember. Or, failing that, invent."

Dance. Embrace. Remember. Invent.

TEMPER *of the* DANCE

Temper of the Dance

for Mangai

anupada
the gods and people dance
while the gods dance the world
in and out of existence
like bees creating and destroying a hive
the people dance stories of love and war
of dharma and betrayal
the dancer transforms
shifting body
changing the temper of the dance

note

anupada: chorus, refrain, burden of a song or words sung again after regular intervals.

dharma can mean many things in Sanskrit. Its general meaning is good or appropriate conduct, but it can also be as strong as law or simply good behaviour.

love

Pūtanā

the world can be lost or made   in the blinking of an eye
in *nangiar koothu*   a dance
of moments   moments between moments
in the lift of an eyebrow   disaster brews
her hand moves   each move tells a story
stories in between
a Russian doll of gestures

Pūtanā's tale is not a pretty one
asked to kill every boy in the land
by King Kaṃsa
an echo of that other king
Herod
never the maternal type Pūtanā
goes about her task until—
until she comes upon Kṛṣṇa
that playful god
in baby form
who strings her along

in a parallel world
a cow suckles her calf

Pūtanā contemplates the unthinkable
to feed this child instead of killing him

fear fills her   fear of King Kaṃsa
not known for   acts of generosity
he'll lop her head   if she does this
she pauses   she watches the cow

indecision

see it — the twinging muscles of her face
each one — separated out
her eyes moving — from compassion to fear
fear to — overwhelming love

audience — mesmerised
still — listening to the muscles move
will she — won't she
will love win — or hatred

poor Pūtanā — gives her hand
to love
to exhilaration

but women in epic and opera die young
Pūtanā for all her consuming hatred
is killed in her moment of love

by a baby
her milk — her life
sucked from her — by Kṛṣṇa

notes

Pūtanā (lit: putrefaction) a rākṣasī or demoness, killed by Kṛṣṇa (Krishna). She is also Kṛṣṇa's foster-mother because she breastfed him, though she had intended to poison him with her breast milk.

Nangiar Koothu is a traditional dance form performed by a woman. Performances are taken from stories depicting the life of Kṛṣṇa using facial expressions, hand gestures and movement accompanied by the mizhavu drum.

King Kaṃsa (Kamsa), a rākṣasa or demon. He hears a prophecy that his cousin Devakī will have a son, Kṛṣṇa, who will kill him. He imprisons Devakī and kills her children but Kṛṣṇa escapes, is raised among cowherds and later kills his uncle Kaṃsa.

Kṛṣṇa (lit: black, dark, dark blue). The eighth avatar of the god Viṣṇu (Vishnu), Kṛṣṇa is a child-god, a trickster, a lover, and a hero.

Kuntī I

this girl has a secret which she holds
so close that no one knows
of the son
her teenage shame
ear born
(that's what they all say)

the river Gaṅgā carried him away
this is Karṇa son of the sun
armoured gold he floats downstream
a dazzling radiance

Kuntī has gods on her side gives birth to a second son
remains
parthenos virgin

then there are the others
she is mother to five sons not counting Karṇa
parthenos Kuntī

having avoided being a single mother the first time round
her husband Paṇḍu suddenly dies she is left
to raise five sons amid widowhood

notes

Kuntī plays a major role in the epic poem Mahābhārata. She is the mother of Karṇa, Yudhiṣṭhira, Bhīma, Arjuna (all different fathers) and stepmother/foster mother to Nakula and Sahadeva.

Gaṅgā: the River Ganges which plunges from heaven to earth.

Karṇa, son of Kuntī with Sūrya (sun), Kuntī's first child.

parthenos: Greek, virgin.

Ambā I

this girl has set her mind   to the future
she knows security   when she sees it
she's here today to choose   her future husband
but fate and   blundering Bhīṣma
have set a different   course

like a game of chance
her life is won in a cast of the die
but she's no shirker in the face of fate
she confronts him says   *not happy*
        I want the other one

Bhīsma seems the proper gentleman
provides an escort   sends her to the one she's chosen
but men are fickle   Śālva will not be her salvation
he says   *Bhīṣma beat me hands down and*
        you were the prize
        back you go girlie

and so she does
but by now Bhīṣma's got himself in a pickle
        he's vowed celibacy

Ambā   pulled
from pillar to post   and back again
her will   gets stronger
        and stronger

note

Ambā is the eldest daughter of King Kāśi (Kashi). She and her sisters are abducted by Bhīṣma (Bhishma), but when she returns to choose Śālva he rejects her.

Draupadī 1

even before Kṛṣṇa is on stage
I am worrying about Draupadī
she's the lynchpin of the story

let me set it out
she marries an eligible young man
that famous archer Arjuna
he does the impossible
shoots an arrow into the eye of a parrot

his equal Karṇa
that unknown son of Kuntī
is excluded from the contest
Draupadī calls him *sūtaputra*
a mere charioteer's son
he cannot
he may not win the hand
of a princess

later he shoots two arrows into two eyes of a parrot
in a single shot

fate opens Kuntī's mouth when Arjuna brings home his
one-arrow-shot-one-eye parrot prize

share the prize with your brothers
she's said it many times before

when gods decree such things
there is no escape

Draupadī has   five husbands
ten hands   one hundred fingers

takes on their interests and passions
becomes the most important person in the household
after her mother-in-law

then the gambling begins
it's Yudhiṣṭhira who gets them into this scrape

he has a problem   a gambling problem
he bets everything
his land   his people
his cattle   his houses
his brothers   himself
and   Draupadī

she is in her room   taking time out
          bleeding time

she is   fetched
hair-dragged   into the assembly
her sari   torn
her body   exposed
to a roomful   of men
none of them   moves
none of them   protests
none of   the five brothers
not a   one

Karṇa says *a ten-handed woman*
is nothing but dirt

Kṛṣṇa Kṛṣṇa calls Draupadī

gods have a bigger view
he creates a deception

so that Draupadī's sari never unwinds
like the magic casket that never empties

note

Draupadī marries Arjuna and finishes up wife to the five Paṇḍava brothers.

sūtaputra: Sanskrit: son of a charioteer.

Kuntī 2

Kuntī is aghast
her implacable sons'
                                        silence
collaborators in shame

they leave the easy life
in sorrow and in exile
to the forest

she is silent about the one
who matters most   Karṇa
three times cursed   his guru
the dead cow's   Brahmin owner
mother earth herself   Bhūmidevī

his fate
in the ten hands   of his brothers

note
Bhūmidevī: lit: earth, mother.

anupada
the gods and people dance
while the gods dance the world
in and out of existence
like bees creating and destroying a hive
the people dance stories of love and war
of dharma and betrayal
the dancer transforms
shifting body
changing the temper of the dance

exile

Draupadī 2

exile is long and love is short
but what is there to tell?
in exile
in the forest
birds
animals
Draupadī's hair matted
                her wild look
                never abating

the boys
those husbands
go hunting
go on treks
enjoy their *rite du passage*

Draupadī cooks
sometimes Kṛṣṇa brings magic
a pot that never empties

but what is there to tell?
in exile
in the forest
birds
animals
Draupadī's hair matted

Karṇa 1

when the right hand is away   the left hand plays
outside the forest realm   Karṇa defeats all

but fate cannot avoid him
his armour is given away
his mother comes too late
he makes too many promises
his chariot will fall
his best weapon used too early
his memory lost when he needs it most
he'll be rendered helpless

Ambā 2

she retires to the forest
she has supporters but nothing helps
only obsessing day in day out
about Bhīṣma's future
it is clear she wants him dead

Bhīṣma's mother Gaṅgā
that great river
hears the rumours
gets in early with her curse

being the mother of all rivers has its benefits

she curses Ambā to be born
woman river on one side of her
the other a paltry forest river
of rocks and sand and dried mud

Ambā is set to see this revenge through
several lifetimes
doing long penance

one day she is granted a god-boon
clear as light she says

I want him dead and I want him dead by my hands
and a new course is set

but what is there to tell?

in exile
there is that final terrible year
of living in disguise

Draupadī 3

she unmats her hair
goes as a supplicant
a veiled beggar

                    to the palace
                    of her shame

a year as handmaid seems forever
makes her see the world with new eyes

one year   one lifetime

Arjuna I

volte-face of Ambā   archer Arjuna becomes a girl
while Ambā the girl   becomes an archer

these are tales of twisted destinies
where people and gods intermingle
the sexes flow across the now-static boundaries
sky and sea cannot be separated
hills and clouds are mistaken for one another

the world is in flux and history
is yet to be made

here is Arjuna doing his level best to make it
to be remembered because the god-child
spoke to him so eloquently

but first he must shed his disguise
his woman's attire with the muscles showing through
he laments that it's a waste
to spend so much time as a woman

what use is it?   I'm good at archery not wiles
meanwhile he flicks a finger turns his wrist
and sticks out one hip in a grimace of imitation

he has been married if sharing your bride
with four right hands and four left hands
can count as matrimony

anupada
the gods and people dance
while the gods dance the world
in and out of existence
like bees creating and destroying a hive
the people dance stories of love and war
of dharma and betrayal
the dancer transforms
shifting body
changing the temper of the dance

war

Kuntī 3

and then war comes

all the sons meet
all six of them
they can't all survive this battle
this warring inside Kuntī

Ambā 3

Ambā transformed in the fire of passion
gets a new body a new life
this girl grows up a tomboy
they encourage her in sports games and archery
at which she excels

they call her Śikhaṇḍī

she out runs
out smarts
out strategises
everyone

this is an old life reborn with purpose

when war comes

Bhīṣma stands on enemy lines

Śikhaṇḍī dresses for battle
wears her biggest shoulders
puts on battledress
crowns her head
with the tallest headdress
she shines like no other warrior
on the field

Bhīṣma recognises her
scorns her says
I'm not fighting a woman
just because she's put on
her brother's battledress

he lowers his guard
and his weapons

whereupon Śikhaṇḍī shoots arrow
after arrow
after arrow

and when she hears him say
as he lies pierced by her arrows
it was that man behind you
who shot these arrows into me
not some girl in dress-ups

she strikes him again with furious arrows

it's all a great play to you Bhīṣma the invincible
but you have met your match in me
so convinced were you that I was just a woman
no man has trained as hard
no man could pierce you with his eyes
no man could see your vulnerability
your over-weaning pride
your time is over now
I will discard these vestments
this armour of splendour
I will discard the accoutrements of war
and watch the waning power of men
a passing yuga
a mere transit

instead I will reclaim the simple life
wrap my body in a single length of cloth
take off to the forest with her by my side
the best part of this great charade

note

Śikhaṇḍī (Shikandi) is born female, raised male and marries the princess of Daśārṇa in today's Northern Madhya Pradesh. There are many variations of this story.

yuga: a very long period of time varying from 432,000 human years to 1,728,000 years. We are currently living in the kaliyuga.

Arjuna 2

bows and arrows are his passion
even beating old Indra of the rainbow
his archery always on display in the sky
Arjuna is fretting for battle and like all men
in serried ranks casting their eye
across the same vision on the other side
his innards turn to water
the war machine never stands still
Arjuna is roused to battle fury
the men around in awe even before he begins
none knowing if they'll see the light of the next day

Karṇa 2

five against one is hardly fair
three curses his chariot falls
his best weapon used too early
his memory lost when he needed it most

Karṇa succumbs

his broken body gold stripped
the sunken sun
Kuntī says *my son*
that boy who floated down the Gaṅgā

Kuntī 4

she has had enough
she gives up all attachment
to human society
turns her back
walks away

Draupadī 4

when dharma is mixed with revenge it's a shame job

after the war   after the shame
Draupadī   is found on a mountain
her clothes in shreds   her mind wandering
her mouth moves   but the sounds are strangled
before they can form words

she accepted fate when it delivered
the five-fingers-equals-one-hand marriage
she shared their ambitions and fears
she learnt archery and all about cows
and horses to encourage her sons

but she cannot forget that awful day
when her body was the crime
they dragged her to the assembly
she tried to cover herself they teased
and shame ran like blood

that five-fingered hand   was deep in its pocket
it was not lifted   it was fingering
the future   with new gambles
she was the booty   her freedom lost
her dignity thrown out   with the dice

Draupadī sits on that mountain the wind
running through her she sings a high lament
her pitch out of the range of speech
each time she tries to utter words the wind
snatches them from the edge of her lips

her god-brother comes to sit next to her
she argues through the wind-blown words
she says *you gods are unfair my shame*
cannot be spoken   turn the world upside down
so the powerless can speak their truths

but the winds come   from all directions
they fill her mouth   with air and whistle
into the god-brother's ear   and when he turns
to look at her to catch   what she is saying
he can see only   the silent moon against ice

Draupadī 5

my worry about Draupadī
is that she is never redeemed

a man called the son of god
is betrayed
abandoned by his disciples
crucified
then worshipped

a woman
is betrayed in a game of chance
publicly humiliated
abandoned
and—

her mother-in-law has the greatest feeling for her

even the storyteller
just the wife

abandons Draupadī
to five brothers
in exile

Draupadī?

Messiah?
blamed for her

betrayal
humiliation
abandonment

anupada
the gods and people dance
while the gods dance the world
in and out of existence
like bees creating and destroying a hive
the people dance stories of love and war
of dharma and betrayal
the dancer transforms
shifting body
changing the temper of the dance

EMBRACE

Śleṣa

a way of writing two meanings at once
a way of reading with flexibility
a train going in two directions
simultaneously

śleṣa comes naturally to lesbians
our codes read this way and that
are you on the upper bunk going east
or the lower bunk going west?

like an MC Escher drawing
one hand draws the other
one hand makes love
the other answers

we embrace our double lives
like actors and their alter egos
some say śleṣa is unnatural
I've heard the same said about us

note

śleṣa (shlesha) in Sanskrit poetry is a way of saying two different sentences whose meaning can be completely distinct. The word śleṣa means embrace.

Fire Gods

the fire gods are winning
it's no longer about sacrifice
and chanting their names
or day by day calling out
for prosperity and health

everywhere and in all directions
the great heat is coming
they come in company with others
storm gods and wind

they used to say that doing homage
in thought alone
would illumine darkness
but those shining herders
no longer pace the sky

Firewalk

in the night a monster a man spiked with
metal rods walking trancing his way across
the coals that monstrous heat but pain
deterred in this place where the sacred and
the jostling crowds meet the whole world
begins to rock like a school of fish everyone
moves at the same strange pace our faces
scorched by heat eyes ablaze in wonder at
this feat that should bring tormented cries
as if a mountain were bleeding lava the
blousy flowers of trees shrivelling the rain
deferred while clouds gather at the horizon's
edge tomorrow will be wet

Two Bright Horses

gallop the curved
space-time
of night
wearing sun shafts
like the variegated splendour
of racing mares
winged
quivering horse sweat
crossing
those eight horns
of earth
infiltrating dark with light

Storm Gods

the storm gods are all
drunkards or on ice
and in their intoxicated state
they make themselves gods

their mother is a cow
in imitation they beautify their bodies
but cannot forget their masculinity
and so they rage

beating up everyone in their path
shaking the mountains
discharging great waters
which are red horses running

intoxication spreads
in a hallucination
giant vultures sit on the grass
as if they are human

monsoon turns to cloudswell
rain plinks
in ancient metrical form
a rāga in flood

Earthsky

earthsky is a haven
for the poet of air
the double dark matter disk
flings celestial bodies
across the solar system

gopī daughters
wild girl gangs
milk the sky cow
running adrift they are
like long-haired comets

note
gopī: Sanskrit: the girls in charge
of herding cows.

AT2018cow

cosmic cow is spinning
so new they hardly know what to say
she has them perplexed stumped flummoxed

Queenie disrupts
it's what she's always done
out in the boon docks of the universe

her brilliance
her magnetic strength
pulsating through the light years

Hercules thought he had her
safely constellated in his dwarf galaxy
but she has exploded into hypermassive luminosity

Queenie says she been here before
but while the earthlings watch and ponder
her internal energy throbs out there flanked by stars

note

AT2018cow: This poem is based on a news item 'Mysterious cosmic 'cow' may have produced a black hole or fast-spinning neutron star'. Astronomers have been chasing 'the cow' for months and have seen nothing else quite like it.

Hercules (also known as Heracles in Greek): Roman hero. He is the son of Alcmene and while in his cradle is reputed to have strangled two serpents sent by the goddess Juno/Hera to kill him.

Queenie is a character from my collection *Cow*. She has a rather long history.

Ancient Cataclysm

worlds on the warpath
earth perturbed
mountains agitated

even the distance
between sky and earth
must be buttressed

they kill snakes
strangle rivers
cows are rustled

clouds are on fire
all is precarious
the old demons

are disappeared
they take all
they devour all

Storm Season

horse clouds
rumble across the sky

the monsoon is a great howler
with arms as hard as

the adamantine
gate of Tartarus

the storm can be tender-
hearted   it carries me

to the far shore   provides
cooling shade in heat

sun bracelets encircle
the raincloud

arcing above the sea
a multicoloured necklace

note

Tartarus: in Greek mythology a
very deep place of torment.

Bṛhaspati's Cows

cows are at the centre of some worlds
take Bṛhaspati who claims to be the first born of all the gods
he has a herd of shining speckled cows
a well-dug well and stones are milked
honey oozes from the earth

Bṛhaspati is born from heaven's light
his seven faces beaming seven rays
with his bellow he blows apart night

he keeps his herd of cows in a cave
drives them up to the air
bellowing all the while with the echo
of a song of praise sung by the following throng

but the first-born god has forgotten
that darkness and caves come before light
that the source is the yoni that brings him to illumination

note

Inspired by *Ṛg Veda* iv.50. Bṛhaspati was a Vedic god associated with the idea of Brahma in all of its meanings, and sometimes the brahmā priest of the gods.

yoni: Sanskrit: womb, uterus, vulva, vagina. Can also mean source, origin, spring as well as grain and a place of rest.

Surabhī and Nandinī

it's a story that can be told in reverse
how we orbit the cosmic cow to solve our aridity
her udder full spilling milk across the sky
her dugs as big as jugs

death is an event on the horizon
when Nandinī enters the Himalayan cave
her bellow reverberates in the hollow
a sound chamber of rumbling echoes

twenty-one days we sleep with her
waiting on this wish-fulfilling cow day and night
the interstellar space between her horns
is a fissure to other worlds

at dusk in the space between light and dark
she shines red like the star on the forehead of Taurus
Rohinī visible in between worlds like the sound
of the wind-fluting bamboo   singing life

walking in the apron of the forest our eyes dry from fasting
flowering trees shower us with falling blossoms
birdsong echoes as the vines hold fast to the trunks
there are many acts of worship for a cow

offer her sweet grasses and scratch her red hide
wave away the flies that settle on her wide shoulders
become her shadow   standing   stopping when she does
move on   sit down   drink water when she does

by these means you will follow the way of the cow
follow in her dusty wake
her four dugs are the four oceans
filled with unending seas of milk

note

This story is drawn from the *Raghuvaṃśa* of Kālidāsa, Cantos 1.88 to 2.38.

Surabhī is the wish fulfilling cow and the mother of all cows. Nandinī is her calf, her daughter. Surabhī is also known as Kamadhenu.

Rohinī is Aldebaran, the brightest star in the constellation of Taurus.

Uṣas

and so this easy daily light in the east
has created clarity from darkness
may the Uṣasaḥ dawning sky daughters
blaze a path for the people

the dazzling Uṣasaḥ have set themselves
in the east glistening like the oiled sacrificial posts
flaring they have unbolted the double doors
of the cowstall of darkness bright and cleansing

in the day's light may Uṣasaḥ munificent ones
resolve to give and give
let the misers sleep in oblivion
unkindled from the depths of darkness

whether Uṣasaḥ the blazing ones
are old friends or new
they are herding many sky cows
their seven mouths shining

for truly you goddesses with your sunhorses
yoked on cue you gallop around the worlds
awake! awake! you cry all you sleeping
two- and four-footed creatures

when and where and which of the ancient ones
ordained the tasks of the sunsmiths
when the dazzling Uṣasaḥ follow their glittering path
they are indistinguishable an eternal haze of light

those ones the inspiring Uṣasaḥ
for whom the sacrificial priestess toils
by recitation singing praise and with healing words
in just a day she obtains wealth

from the east they come all the same
spreading light all the same
those waking goddesses are like a rush of cows
the Uṣasaḥ on the move

all the same these same-coloured Uṣasaḥ
are on the move they hide the black monster
of night with their incandescent bodies
showering blazing beams sun shafts

sun daughters Uṣasaḥ while showering us
with light will your gifts extend to wealth and children?
our eyes sun drenched we wake to you
from our sunlit bed

I sing to you sun daughters Uṣasaḥ
with your blazing forms
wishing for fame if only
heaven and goddess earth will give it

note

I have made this translation based on *Ṛg Veda* Uṣas Book iv:51.

Uṣas is the preeminent goddess in the *Ṛg Veda and* a goddess of dawn. Uṣas is associated with cows and in the *Ṛg Veda* she is called the mother of cows. Her Proto-Indo-European name has given many other words in Indo-European languages including Éos (Greek), Aurora (Latin), Ausrine (Lithuanian) and probably Eostre (the root of English Easter). Uṣasaḥ plural form, is Uṣas in her multiple aspect.

Twenty stanzas of *Meghadūta*

a whole year passed and the Yakṣa pined
though he lived in pleasant surrounds
among Rāmagiri's shady trees
and the holy waters of Sītā
yet still he ached
only himself to blame for Kubera's curse

his mind bent by longing for her
love bangle slipped from his famished arm
with bittersweet pangs of love
he hungered on that lonely mountain top
on a windy day portending monsoon
he saw an elephant cloud rutting the cliff face

his yearning peaked as he stood
before this phantasm of elephant
dry-eyed tears welling inside
even the cheerful mind is ruffled
by the sight of a rough-skinned cloud
he wished his arms a necklace

as the month of śrāvaṇa approached
the month of listening he prepared
to send news through the cloud ear
he made an offering of fresh kudaja flowers
spoke aloud his words filled with love
sustenance for his beloved

his mind bent by yearning
he clutches at cloud elements
vapour light water wind
mistakes cloud breath for vital breath
poor lovelorn Yakṣa can't sense
the mirror from its reflection

Yakṣa speaks to the cloud saying
I know you are born into the world-wandering
shapeshifting clan related to thunder-bearing
Indra I call on you to help me most lofty one
my kin are far away and destiny tells me
to make a humble request though it be futile

rain-giver you are a refuge in sticky heat
Kubera has parted me from my beloved
and I beg that you travel to her in Alakā
with my message where you'll find a palace
bathed in the light of a crescent moon on the head
of Śiva standing in the outer garden

ascend the path of the wind sky-fly
so the wives need no longer sigh
at their unravelled hair imploring
their well-travelled husbands to return
whereas I in thrall to Kubera
have neglected my beloved

without obstruction follow the jet stream
how you float unlike my beloved
her heart like a wilted flower
she needs the thread of hope
to buoy up her spirits in fruitless
counting of days and nights

as the wind drives you slowly slowly
the cātaka bird sings sweetly sweetly
skeins of cranes are in flight
cloud seeded they fly in formation
like a garland aloft pleasing to
the sky-turned eye

your sky companions the gander kings
have heard your thundering gait
they long for Lake Mānasa so high
they watch for mushrooming earth
and carry food strips of lotus root
as you fly together to Mount Kailāsa

lofty mountain embraced by cloud
rain tears and farewells marked
by Rāmagiri's receding footprints
steaming tears stream down
the mountain's face a knot
of loss born of long separation

oh cloud listen to me
let your ears be drunk
on sound   listen follow
the path laid down
drink from bubbling streams
rest when exhausted

beneath you bewildered
women watch the crowd
of elephant clouds a   shiver
of north wind carries off
the mountain tusk
beware the quarter elephants

face-to-face a sliver of Indra's
bow rises from the anthill
a kaleidoscope of colours
in crystalline refraction
your indigo body glittering
like a glamour of peacocks

fruits of harvest grown
on moisture from you
fertile as the wombs
of women sweet sacred
smell of turned earth
climb the brow to the cloud-road

ride the spine of Āmrakūṭa
the ground awash with
your downpour extinguishing
wildfire such kindness is
returned providing refuge
for high flying friends

cloud braid lies along Āmrakūṭa's
spine fringed with mango orbs
the mountain a curve of breast
its dark nipple in the middle
a coupling of gods looks
at the pale vastness of earth

the young wives of forest nomads
frolic in thick mountain arbours
you sprint the rim of mountain
streams riven by strewn boulders
like the cross-hatched pattern
decorating the body of an elephant

you whose rain is shed drink
the must-infused water of wild
elephants water-clumped
jambū trees obstruct your way
the wind cannot lift a solid mass
a void is light fullness is gravity

notes

Kālidāsa's *Meghadūta* (*Cloud Messenger*) from approximately the 4th century CE is a poem of 111 stanzas. This poem is based the first 20 stanzas of the poem in Sanskrit. *Meghadūta* is one of several lyric poems by Kālidāsa who wrote three plays as well as epic poems. He is one of the most important poets writing in Classical Sanskrit. Translating Sanskrit provides many challenges, and in this version I take poetic licence in order to make the poem work in English. The Sanskrit metre in which it is written is mandākrānta, a slow elegiac metre.

Yakṣa: a generally benevolent nature spirit.

Rāmagiri: giri: mountain.

Sītā: a foundling, regarded as daughter of Bhūdevī, the earth goddess. Sītā's name means furrow or the line of a ploughshare. A principle character in the epic Rāmāyaṇa.

śrāvaṇa: Sanskrit: the fifth month, July-August.

Kubera: the god of wealth.

Indra: thunder god.

Āmrakūṭa: a mountain.

Sarasvatīkaṇṭhābharaṇa: Sarasvatī's Necklace

so you who are to blame for all the world's ills

you who dance in ever expanding spirals
turning the universe on a point

you who speak as if you are the world's know-all

you whose smallest lapse becomes earth's fault line

you who sweep the sea's tides into our arms

you whose hair is a chaos of cunning

you who cut the layers of learning with your eye

you whose boat hides behind clouds or is starlit

you for whom we sing a never-ending cycle of song

you for whom the snakes and bees dance

your sacraments are our lives

your river is a necklace of ponds

you moon-carrier   sky-wanderer

no weapon is greater than you

notes

Sarasvatī is the Hindu goddess of knowledge, writing, music, art and wisdom. Her name comes from *saras* which can mean both speech and pooling water and *vati*, she who possesses.

The Sanskrit title can be broken down as Sarasvatyāḥ kaṇṭhe ābharaṇam which means ornament on the neck of Sarasvatī.

Notes towards a Poem about Madhu / Honey Demon

Madhusūdana   killer of Madhu
Madhuripu   enemy of Madhu

these are the names of Kṛṣṇa
who is Madhu?

and why does Kṛṣṇa
hate him or her so much?

Madhu   progenitor / springtime
madhu   first month   the season of spring

Madhava the name of spring
spring brings forth her glory

she is fruitful   she is honey-dewed
she is sprung with life   Mādhava

madhu   honey
mādhukara   honey maker / bee

madhu as sweet as honey   lip-licking sweet
the bee dancing like a lover

the sun rising out of winter
the bee rising from the flower

mādhura   sweet
madhuram   sweetly

sweet honey melody	a rāga played
below the horizon	a dance spun

like honey's drop	how sweet is that?
killing love killing	sweet
honey spring?

Madhu	demon
Madhumathana	tormentor of Madhu

Kṛṣṇa tormentor, whose sweet life will you take?
has the bee stung your lip? the honey *prized*

raw food of old mother forest caught you in a trap?
oh honey murderer will the season end?

notes

madhu: means honey or sweet and is related to the English word *mead.*

Madhusūdana: another name for the god Viṣṇu, Kṛṣṇa is associated with the name Madhusūdana because he is an incarnation of Viṣṇu.

Lagna

an imaginary line—aligned—that the lagna poet speaks each morning the lagna's task to watch the sun rise   to wait for that moment when the line of the sun on the horizon intersects the ecliptic—at that moment the poet sings the imaginary line the poetry created for the king's waking the poet oversees the transformation crucial to the king's day from below the line to above the line—this is poetry's accountancy—a decisive moment in the day's passage a time to fix upon auspicious action a time to beware penetrating the heart—the lineage of lagna is fixed by an imagined past of intersecting lines of poetry and planets each following closely on the heels of the other

note

Among the many meanings of *lagna* in Sanskrit are the following: a bard or minstrel who wakes the king in the morning; the point of contact or intersection of two lines.

Pooja Rooms

the gods gather this time in sixes
they are the family gods passed down
generation to generation
there in front of the three old trees
are their ancestor gods sitting
beneath the pink and yellow painted trunk

here are the idols all bronzed and golden
tucked up in heaps of rice
a bowl of milk and sweetwater next to it
one tends to the gods and their needs
just as one tends a garden
feed and water daily speak to them
listen to their whispering sounds

here the names are changed it's
Murugan and Pillaiyer the elephant one
as well as Saraswati and Meenakshi
fish-eyed and a sextet of gods
all leaning in the same direction
eyeing the six-faced Arumuga

the candle is lit the coloured lights blink
there is something precious about these
small shrines to daily devotion
it's not my way but I feel something
flicker something shimmer
at the edge of my consciousness

notes

Murugan: also known as Kārttikeya, the name Murugun, the youth, is used in Tamil speaking areas. He is sometimes depicted with six heads for the six mothers of the Pleiades who raised and cared for him as a baby.

Pillaiyar: a south Indian god, similar to Gaṇeśha, the elephant-headed one, who is the brother of Kārttikeya.

Saraswati: Tamil spelling of Sarasvatī.

Meenakshi: a goddess whose name means fish-eyed. The huge Meenakshi Temple in Madurai is dedicated to her.

Arumuga: another name for Murugan.

Trijaṭā's Dream

don't listen to the propaganda of my brother
he's a fool
his head has grown long
his arms short
he thinks that sword will save him

I've seen her dressed in moonlight
on a milk-drenched mountain
above a foaming sea
eight white bulls draw her forward
across the sky

she touches the moon with her hand
everything shines
her face
her flying chariot
the cloud-shrouded peak

my brother is earth and dung-smeared
his skin blooming red
hair dragging mud
that heart of his
is a clot of blood

note

Trijaṭā is a female rākṣasī (or demon) who comforts the goddess Sītā during her imprisonment by Rāvaṇa, the demon king of Laṅkā. The story appears in Vālmīki's *Rāmāyaṇa*.

SAPPHO'S BUTTERFLY

Sappho's butterfly

I'm twenty-two when I'm kissed by Sappho's butterfly
at nine I vow not to marry before twenty-three

I wake with the word *nabiwindward* in
my mind   she said   *nahbee*   it means butterfly in
Korean   it's many-coloured   *poikilothron* and as artful
as a spider cunning and all knowing—we ask one

another riddles we speak in codes and tell stories
I tell you about Aphrodite   she's no nymph she's as
ancient as sea and sun   rising from the sea with
the sun upon her brow the ocean melting

she's no maniac and mortality   she says   is for the birds

in spite of our low birth rate and centuries of
persecution we've never been eliminated
poikilothron athanata is Sappho's name for
Aphrodite—the many-coloured deathless calls

of love   at the centre of the universe is a giant egg—
was it swans or ostriches   emus or cassowaries
who laid the original egg? *I don't care* you say as
your child legs carry you away from the chasing swans—

and on your face a look of shocked surprise
did you know that Komodo dragons can do parthenogenesis?
that old virgin birth trick again   on a cold autumn
night a full moon rises over your dead brother's grave

the church spire is glowing—floodlit it lifts rising above
the body of the church   so many years so much time
but when I re-meet the spurned lover there's a moment of
shock while I realign myself and see once again the moss-

green hat of the woman on the plane   feel the cold in
my bones as I wake on the carpet at dawn before the
burnt out fire   a letter from my friend in Tonga who is
listening to the fairy tales of turtles and swimming in a

bottomless pool diving deep   surfacing for air and more stories

on a winter solstice day I eat three mushrooms
ambrosia and call on Aphrodite and Circe
no wallowing in a pigsty for me no swill just the
dance   the laughing flutes and transformation

notes

nabi (pronounced: nahbee), Korean: 나비

poikilothron: Greek: many coloured.

athanata: Greek: undying.

Aphrodite: Greek goddess of love, but her origins are far more ancient, likely connected to the Middle Eastern goddesses Astarte and Ishtar.

Circe is the daughter of Helios, the Greek sun god and aunt of Medea, daughter of King Aeëtes of Colchis.

Things a Lesbian Should Know

that the lesbian is as old as humanity—and maybe older
how to conjugate the verb to love in any tongue

the walls of my cell are high
the stones thick   the time I've been here
immeasureable   millennia

                                        I am a political
prisoner and my crimes are made of love

we walked under the cedar trees
outside the walls of the city
we kissed as the new moon set
as if time were going backwards

we troubled no one in the quietness
of our passion   our robes hiding
our faces   the near dark obscuring
our movements   our tears

as the sun rose we sang love songs
to one another as we prepared to part

then they came   the horsemen
wielding lances   tearing at our clothes
hauling us up behind them
we were abducted   raped   beaten   imprisoned

                                        why?   we cried
for your crimes   they said

they would not allow us to speak
neither on our own behalf   nor to
question their decisions   and so we languish
no one has begun a campaign to free us

the people say   *why should we help them?*
they are abhorrent   they are vile

every few centuries we slip out into the world
they no longer remember we are here

when we escape we find others
we create circles of passion
we shout our anger in those same streets
near where we were once abducted

soon the horsemen come again
each time we are arrested the weaponry
has advanced   vast investment and political will
fastened into every notch.

we have been strung up on pulleys
our fingers broken   we have been burnt
we have been drowned and declared innocent
we have been shot through with electrical charges

whipped, stoned and thrown from buildings
we have been drugged with every known poison
and on each occasion we are raped

for your own good   they say

the walls have not fallen
we prisoners still communicate
by tapping our fingers against the walls
today they told me that forever was over

but I know better   I know them in ways
they cannot imagine
the walls of my cell are high
but as before   I will keep on escaping

Nonsense

I am a nonsense
I do not exist

or if I do I am illegal
and should be punished

killed if need be
in Hunan China my words

are hidden in nüshu
in my own land

like so many others
silence is preferred

self-suffocation of words
my history is full of

horizontal lines but
none are vertical

my position in the family
is at the far end

of a fragile twig ready
to break from the main stem

in the desert lands
my bones are broken

whipped into the centre
of a sand storm

vanished as if I have
never existed

under dictatorships
I am among the first

to be crushed
my independence

my nonsense
a threat to social stability

I am pushed from the trapdoor
of a plane no parachute

to break my fall
only the sea to catch me

in its hardened arms
in the cold lands

they call me an artist
sell my soul to that grumpy

old Mephistopheles
who's never satisfied

no matter how far I go
I remain exotic

a work of theatre
at the centre of empire

words are decorated
with ribbons of acceptance

dissertations are mined
to snuffle out meaning

there's betrayal in those awards
in so many places records

are changed the archaeologies
rebuilt and reshaped

to other realities
today I was murdered

by someone sent by
the government

note
nüshu: a script from Shangjiangxu, a small part of southwestern Hunan Province in China, used exclusively by women.

Sense

I am sense
I exist in the most complete

way I can I walk with joy
using every muscle in my body

to express vitality
in China we are coming out

of laneways to waltz
daily on the Bund in Shanghai

I teach the young where she
should put her hand

how to find the rhythm
in the bones of her feet

I speak of my self   breathing
words into her ear while

walking down the street
my genealogy is recorded

and we visit the place of
our ancestors weaving silk

making rituals of hair
licking the juice of sweet mango

I climb the family tree and
sit firmly in the Y of the trunk

some go this way others that
the deserts when you look

when you really feel
are already so full of life

the dictatorships? the young
ask for the meaning of such words

for they have vanished as
completely as those they once

disappeared I take flight
at times of my choosing

parachuting into love
the sea's arms a caress

my art is my own drawn
from the heart the hand

our worlds flourish not
because of some reward

but because we are human
in these worlds our histories

and archaeologies
are celebrated for the

richness they prove
that lies in each of us

Patriarchal Grammar

a way of knowing that all you know
is all there is to know

a way of speaking so that everyone
else knows to remain silent

a way of being that lets you walk through life
oblivious to the pain of others

a way of making asymmetric war
against the powerless

a way of using your body as a weapon
and then calling it love

Cyane

moon pool   colour code for blue
Cyane is older than us all
river home for a Sicilian nymph

but she was no nymphette
she stood up to the death god
abducting her friend Proserpine

called out to him *stop   this is no way*
to gain a wife let her go   Pluto
in self-rapture ruptured earth

Cyane stood in silence   wept
and wept yet more   with each
new tear her body dissolved into fluid

her hair blue as the sea melted
limb by limb shoulder by arm
she wasted away in grief for her friend

when Ceres arrived all speech
had been swallowed into liquid
no words just bubbling and burbling

but she showed to Ceres the sash
of Proserpine and Ceres knew
the truth of her daughter's abduction

in Syracuse they remember Cyane
her transformation her metamorphosis
from young girl to sacred blue river

notes

Inspired by Book V of Ovid's *Metamorphosis*.

I have used the Roman names for the Greek gods in keeping with Ovid's use. Proserpine is Persephone; Pluto is Hades; Ceres is Demeter.

Proserpine/Persephone is the daughter of Ceres/Demeter. Proserpine becomes Queen of the Underworld after she is abducted and raped by Pluto/Hades.

The Clamping of Alcmena

childbirth is a battleground
the powerful on one side
women and midwives on the other

philandering Jove made Alcmena
a single mother and Juno
wanted her revenge

the child to be Hercules
grew big too big for poor Alcmena
to deliver with ease

but worse was Juno's plotting
with Lucina gatekeeper between
uterine darkness and light of birth

Lucina in the palm of Juno sits
as tight as a Gordian knot
limbs interwoven fingers

like hands knitted
Alcmena labours seven days
hoarse with pain almost dead

her midwife and maid Galanthis
saw Lucina's tightening grip
sees through the charade

she makes her own play
cheering Alcmena's long agony
it is over she is delivered

astonished Lucina frees her
fingers unwinds her legs
and the child is released

Galanthis poor woman pays
for her loyalty metamorphosed
her arms now animal forelegs

her gold hair short and rough
in her weasel form   Alcmena
loyal too holds her as her familiar

notes

Inspired by Book 9 of Ovid's *Metamorphosis*.

Galanthis was turned into a weasel, cat or lizard depending on the story.

Circe

it's a circle
her home a palindrome
Aeaea ends as it begins

perhaps that's as it is
with the creatures that roam
around her house

they are softies in the bodies
of wolves and pigs
fawning in visitors' laps

Circe was no fool
no greater expert was there
in pharmacopoeia

her powers transformative
turning men to beasts
and beasts to men

she's reinvented herself
circling in space dark
asteroid 34

notes
Circe is conventionally referred to as a witch. By this we can assume that she was a woman of great power who understood medical preparations. Circe appears in *The Odyssey* by Homer. Emily Wilson's new translation of *The Odyssey* is a fine new interpretation in which the role of women is neither minimised or reduced to sexist stereotypes.

Fragment 16, Sappho

some say an army of horses some say an army of feet
some say an army of ships is the most beautiful thing
on this black earth but I say it is whom-
ever you love

easy to make this thought catch
for she who was more beautiful
than all humanity
left her sublime husband behind

to sail to Troy
neither children nor loved parents
could she perceive
but deceived—she went

for
lightly
recall to me now Anaktoria
no longer here

note

Sappho was an Aeolian poet, born between 630 and 612 BCE on Lesbos off the coast of modern-day Turkey.
She died around 570 BCE. She invented lyric poetry and the myxolydian musical mode and wrote many songs and poems in Aeolic Greek.

Fragment 22, Sappho

deeds
limb test ...
cry out
if not wintry torment
ruthless

sing of
Gongyla   Abanthis   grasp
the harp – and again – longing
wafts all around

your loveliness for when you saw her
garment you were excited
and I thrilled

Cyprus-born Aphrodite condemned me
for praying one word:
want

note

Anne Carson in *If not, winter: Fragments of Sappho* (2003, note 22.10 p. 363) writes that Gongyla means yoke-mate. In Sanskrit the root verb √yuj means to yoke, harness or fasten. It can be applied to two cows yoked together; it can also mean unite or connect in a relationship or through longing. Carson says the first two letters of Gongyla's name are missing from this poem. Sanskrit for cow is gau/go-: go-. Are the two missing letters like the lesbians missing from history?

Five Rivers

I. Acheron

finding my way through
the five rivers
of the underworld
not easy to navigate
paradise might not be within reach
I ask   whose paradise is it?

before I enter the underworld
I talk to Charon
that old ferryman
an equal opportunity program
has been in place
it's a ferrywoman this time
she's taken the old name
has to   comes with the job
she ferries me across the Acheron
I weep and weep
and weep some more
a lake of tears
the woes of all
who have died before

2. Cocytus

the river Acheron is not enough
by the time Charon
drops me on the bank
between the Acheron
and the Cocytus
I am wailing and lamenting
everything I've done wrong
I am calling out for the lost ones
those poisoned or shot

who would have known
I had so many tears in me?
tears like blood
bursting from me

3. Phlegethon

our boat has gone round in a circle
returned to the Acheron
it meets its tributaries
Phlegethon
and Periphlegethon
air fills with a miasma of smoke
my eyes run not with tears of sorrow
but from canisters of tear gas
hurled at me
the way is slow as we
circumnavigate
these two endless rivers
I sleep for an unknown time

4. Styx

the river Styx is commanded
by the goddess of the same name
she is a feisty one
so much so that an oath
made to her is unbreakable
whether you be immortal
or a deity
I make dozens of oaths of revenge
if Styx is on my side
I'll be like that old fart Achilles
invulnerable
that's if you believe it
for now   I will

5. Lethe

we are soon swooning
along a swollen Lethe
I dunk my bottle into its waters
drunk on oblivion
I forget my losses
my tears and lamentations
my oaths of revenge
later much later I will drink
with Mnemosyne

note

Mnemosyne is the mother of the nine Muses. She is the goddess of memory and daughter of Gaea (Earth) and Uranus (Sky).

The SACKING *of the* MUSES

01 The Sacking of the Muses

the Muses have been sacked
their role in the pantheon
sold up for some new
real estate venture

the Muses have fled
all nine of them
in a mathematical
and artistic frenzy

they are downcast
what's a Muse to do
to amuse herself
in these penny-pinching days?

how can a poet expect
to have her work
taken seriously when
profit is deemed all?

the Muses are unemployed
on the dole living
on the smell of an oily rag
their hearts raging

02 Kalliope, Muse of Epic Poetry

I'm drawn to Kalliope who can sing for days
her verses flowing without end
one night I sat by her as she sang
her epic poems to the stars
she says they are not so long
not even a light year song
they are intricate their metre complex
and rhythmic so you can dance

as she sang it seemed that the stars came closer
the trees huddled around us and the whispers
of animals could be heard in the forest
before I knew it I could hear the rushing sound
of a stream just out of reach
I listened and watched the night through
I woke to the sound of a trumpeting swan
the clatter of grasshopper wings

03 Muses are Organising

the Muses are organising
they have always been a collective
and this time is no different

Kalliope arrives first   eldest
of the sisters she is always in the lead
the others follow talking about the news

not only have we been sacked
it's worse they have decided not
to recognise us at all

white-anting the arts
you can't see us any more
we don't exist can't be discussed

do these governments know nothing?
you can't decide not to know about
music poetry song dance

our domains of tragedy and comedy
could embrace this policy if only
they could see and hear us

they know nothing of history
history is what happened ten minutes ago
in a newsroom in America

in spite of rockets and space probes
they have thrown out astronomy
hobbled by her old cousin astrology

time to call up the tenth Muse
Sappho the world has turned
and we do remember you

04 Polyhymnia, Muse of Song

I thought Polyhymnia would be a walk over
a softie away with the fairies   her head
in the clouds but this Muse is serious

she is sacred through and through
whether it be poetry hymns or dance
its her eloquence that lifts her and us

she is solid too in her farm boots
turning the soil following the ox-plough
digging weeding and harvesting

then come the celebrations of harvest
pantomimes for which you need
geometry to organise a stage

Polyhymnia is queen of silence
meditation more than a hobby
on Parnassus she listens to the

oracles of Pythia nothing is lost
it was her son Orpheus who picked up
the lyre and revived the dead

05 Muses are Grieving

all our dead are beside us
the humans dogs cats
and other familiars
those for whom I have no body
are memory holes
how to contain grief with words
with calmness with love
or something else
something not yet known

in grief the dead become undead
we tell stories though some names
are too raw to speak out loud
an eyeless seizure
taut as a violin string
howls splintering
the cold night air

history erases us
Syria trembles with new wars
over old enmities ancient Isis
replaced by misnamed acronym
warmongers misogynists

there are no antediluvian
antipathies just common loss
its ritual agonies of unbidden tears
lamentations of the body
regrets for time lost
a place in which dance is sacred

even the screeches of cockatoos
the bleaches of coral reefs
poignant pain of artists
singers and poets
writing hermetic sigils in dust
these are mnemonics
for future generations
so that histories might be told

the shock and loss and pain
that leaves you reeling
psyche with metamorphic ache
grief creates culture
when written words are absent
recall is preserved in stories

places visited
memories as treasure
stories become song
chant turns to dance
images drawn on rocks
and sand represent
the loved ones
we raise our stooping
shoulders and begin to dance

06 Melpomene, Muse of Tragedy

in your boots you stomp around the stage
with your knife your club and that hideous mask
life is tragic enough without making it ugly too

your sting is like that of the bee whose honey
is sweet but the bite can kill that's how the tragic
arts are   we are all engrossed in the story

meanwhile our lover has died of heartbreak
or lost dreams or serial disappointments
we all think we are immune to tragedy in our lives

until it strikes without warning like lightning flash
there is no way back we are all changed
by those moments when we had hoped for joy

Melpomene sing your dirges for me so that
I might haul myself up unwrap the cloths
split the hard chrysalis emerge transformed

07 Muses in Hiding

the Muses have gone into hiding
on the day after 11/9
they say it's no longer safe
this might be too paranoid
but they say they have seen it before
don't worry said the nice men
some six thousand years ago
everything will be fine
provided you stay polite
don't wind them up with your rituals
go along with this single god thing
what is one god against you
nine Muses and all your sister
goddesses everything will be fine

the Muses have retreated to the caves
the distant hills the hidden valleys
the underground bars
all the places invisible to men
they say they need to gather their strength
sing dance write poetry and songs
they need to gaze at the stars
retell their histories in prose and poetry
they will be performing their rituals
as the need arises and when the time is right

08 Ourania, Muse of Astronomy

Ourania is an enigma
she is invisible in her starry robe
against the darkening sky
but each clear night we stand
watching her movements

darkness is in her she is
the dark matter that fills
the universe the dark energy
that sparks everything

in daylight she has a golden
orb around her as she rides
the sky in a boat laden
with songs carries a globe
constantly spinning

Ourania full of magic
is the first astronomer
Uranian once considered
a tragic pronouncement

who knows what goes on
in that heavenly soul
she is old and young
she is light years away
and right here now

just as we are here
and are everywhere
but in fireworks of celebrity
unseen unheard unknown

09 Muses Undercover

speaking otherwise
reading slant knowing
the view from below
even sideways is useful

when you go undercover
best disguise is normality
be a daddy's girl if need be
then you can unwork
the system as Valerie said

we are in every workplace
in the spaces of family trees
some without issue others
bedded even more deeply

when you go undercover
don't forget who you are
we want you back after
the crisis is over remember
you are no slave to them

10 Erato, Muse of Lyric Poetry

everything always lovely
her eyes her hair the way
she moves her body

Erato is like the sea
washing up on the shore
rising and falling in waves

poets call on Erato in their
darkest moments when love
turns sour or the stars cross

and when inspiration fails
they call her then hoping
she'll stand by them in love and lyric

it's partly her fault because she
shoots words into the sky
like arrows and whoever

feels those arrows falls in love
with the next person they encounter
but who can get angry with Erato?

so full of grace she picks up her lyre
sings with a voice that is as clear
as a night sky filled with stars

11 Muses Writing a Manifesto

Erato says she loves a spot
of weaving texts   back in her day
a text was a woven thing
words braided and interwoven

while not much into
writing manifestoes
she says she'll join in
so long as the manifesto
begins with poetry

in poetry we have depth
twisted in with memory
what use is a manifesto
you can't remember by heart?

Erato is plucking words
she is feeling the rhythms
she needs when she finishes
her spinning and weaving
she will share words with us

12 Kleio, Muse of History

when history is in dispute
who can you trust but Kleio?
she was there and if not her
then one of her sisters
her kinship is wide enough
to draw in the world

it's not in the telling
but in the unravelling
who speaks true who does not
one will claim celebrity status
say fame is the key to import
another says the least known

are the most trustworthy
for they have nothing
to gain or to lose
the poets too stay firm
to their metre there since
the beginning of time

history in the making
is a troublesome way to go
for only later can we see
the made and the unmade
so unravel your tales
and I will weave them anew

13 Muses are Occupying

we move in under cover of darkness
with our blankets for the night
and sun hats for the day

we are occupying the up-market
end of town where star arts
happen under the guise of excellence

the star arts receive funding
every year   they drink cocktails
they appear on television screens

we look like a bunch of hobos
we've come a long way
up from the dark caves

where we've been meeting
these last weeks so our rustic
attire is intentional

we say we represent
the arts at the edge of chaos
well beyond your horizon

in the darkest hour of the night
we begin our chant we draw
the spirit of rebellion to us

by morning all that is left
are a few leaves some woven threads
butterfly wings and small red hearts

14 Euterpe, Muse of Music

Euterpe is in her own heaven
the fifth dimension where
beyond human perception
play the music of the spheres
music from every time
and every place

Euterpe is well schooled
in these matters
she is the muse of music
music creates pleasure
which in turn leads
us to dance

some think Euterpe
is connected to asteroid
27 Euterpe one of the
brightest asteroids
in the solar system
Pythagoras

gave Euterpe the number
eight that coiling infinity
ogdoad like a dancer
endlessly spinning
to the sound of
the double flute

astrophysicists
are divided some
think Euterpe might
be responsible for dark
matter but some things
are unaccountable

15 Muses Love Pageants

out of the fifth dimension
a stream of music unheard
for six thousand years

dingoes approach
padding along in a pack
little ones in the middle
elders at the front

sounds break into scraps
voice here song there
tambourines and clapsticks

Suzanne is leading the pageant
words escape their chains
they are being used to mean
things they've never meant before

on the other side of the bushes
is a herd of cows who were heard
to moo throughout the whole show

16 Thalia, Muse of Comedy

it's hard to be funny
when Thalia abandons you
but each of us has to get up
draw on inner reserves
and make one more joke

Aristophanes managed it
and you can too   bring on
actors and instead of high
boots make them wear socks
dress like country bumpkins

put a shepherd's crook in
their hands – I know more than
enough about droving sheep
to laugh at myself – then she
can start her bucolic verses

accompanied by comedic
flourishes a few stereotypes
here and there won't go astray
put a buffoon at the centre
and her air-head husband

he can parrot some phrases
give the quiet one a trumpet
to blow away sadness
don't worry there will be
a happy ending now sing

along with me it's simple
tiotiotiotinx sing again
the bird never tires calling
sing blow that trumpet
recite the verse and be happy

17 Muses are Dancing

dance dance dance
dance the trata in your
red white and black garb
dive down dive down
dive underground

dance dance dance
dance the trata
for bread and pomegranate

dance as we have
for millennia
as is carved
on the tomb
of the dancing women

dance a zigzag
dance the weave of a basket
dance the stars and spirals
        inwards
        outwards

enter the labyrinth
with the young ones leading
dance as if your life depends
on the dance

sing with the old ones
sing out your strong voices
voices that hold the world
sing like swallows
twittering to bring spring

dance dance dance
sing sing sing
dance the trata
sing the spring

18 Terpsichore, Muse of Dance

I write in fragments
because that is how
our history is recorded
whether it's Sappho
Corinna or Roman
Sulpicia

Corinna is called
by Terpsichore to sing
for the young girls
women of Tanagra
wear the white peplos
their

garments are ornamented
with stories tales from
the old mothers
the girls dance to the
partheneia calling one
another

sounds whirling down
the valleys to the
rivers below the cliffs
their voices rising
to heights where
birds fly

grasshoppers
spring and spin
in death throes
returning after death
to the Muses'
home

there sit the Muses
each with her own
sphere Terpsichore
brought the Sirens
into the world
singing

she is the ennead
containing others
she turns gathering
all in her dance
ending the beginning
beginning the end

notes

Corinna of Tanagra in Boeotia who was a lyric poet in the sixth century BCE.

Sulpicia, a Roman poet and author of six extant poems written around 10 BCE.

partheneia: Greek: a chorus of song sung by virgins.

19 Muses Come out of Hiding

we come out of the desert
we carry desert fruits
animal friends accompany us

we are not in hiding
we have never hidden
it is you who could not see

20 Tenth Muse, Sappho

your most recent poems
still make the headlines Psappha
we cite you we remember your lines
and as you'd hoped
someone in some future time
will remember me

we lesbians never believed
the rumours of suicide
from the Leucadian cliffs
we now know that *old age*
has taken its pleasure
turning my black hair white

your ten thousand poems
are fragments shards
of their former selves
your history like so many
to be read in the gaps
in the spaces between the lines

I first read you as lines of graffiti
in the smallest room where
someone wrote *the most beautiful*
thing on this black earth [is]
whomever you love
for you it was Anaktoria

as the moon rises and sets
I think of you yet again
like so many poets
even more lesbians
whose hearts you
awakened and thrilled

notes

Anaktoria, a companion of Sappho/Psappha who is mentioned in Sappho's love poems.

Lines in italics are translations of Sappho's poems by the author. Her poem about old age was found in 2004.

MNEMOSYNE

The Festival of Memoria

the crowds are gathering for the Festival of Memoria
here are the card sharps and memory champions
who'd been dropouts before the crash
the old woman who held all the remedies in her mind
her knowledge of uncultivated plants encyclopaedic
she has created a collective of spinsters
and invited the young healers to join
in the next tent are the gardeners gatherers and cooks
portions of food and potions for the body
the old peoples shine with their astronomical knowledge
they come from the deserts and rainforests
grasslands and shorelines
all night they sing and dance
the great sharing of knowledge now an emergency
all the electronic libraries have gone
there are still books held on shelves
but no one can afford to read them
the libraries were sold by corrupt governments
cash-strapped and myopic
like the rich in their castles when the plague came
some starved for lack of farming knowhow
they are locked in mausoleums of silence
the Festival of Memoria is the new life
it is also the old life regained

here are the keepers of the khipu
the chanters of subhāṣitāni
the knotters and singers
even the knitters and embroiderers
of old memory patterns
canvasses are laid on the ground
each takes her position and paints the world
on the periphery sit the human dictionaries
sharing words for food and fine conversation
here are those who are multilingual
remembering new and old twists of tongue
some are poets who can recite the histories
others are players of tragic and comic forms
it is odd
these days all the old arts have returned
from the woodwork have emerged the reviled ones
who kept them alive without reward
we live within the story
we have our tools our skin feet legs hands arms
bellies larynx nose ears brains
our planet is in good minds

Acknowledgements

2019 Surabhī and Nandinī. *Australian Poetry Anthology,* edited by Yvette Holt and Magan Magan. Vol 7, 2019, p. 100.

I wrote 'The Sacking of the Muses' sequence during 2016 on Project 365+1 which involved writing and uploading a poem every day for a year. Some poems in the section Embrace were also published on Project 365+1 during 2016. <http://project365plus.blogspot.com.au>

Parts of 'The Sacking of the Muses' sequence have been published in a number of different versions.

2019 Nine Muses, Daughters of Mnemosyne. In *She Rises: What Goddess Feminism, Activism and Spirituality?* (Volume 3), edited by Deanne Quarrie and Helen Hye-Sook Hwang. Mago Books.

2018 The Nine Muses, Daughters of Mnemosyne. *Return to Mago, E-Magazine.* <https://www.magoism.net/2018/02/poetry-the-nine-muses-daughters-of-mnemosyne-by-susan-hawthorne/>

2017 The Muses are Dancing and The Tenth Muse, are included in my novel *Dark Matters* (Spinifex Press) as are references to the Mother of the Muses, Mnemosyne, and a variation on Five Rivers.

2017 Sacking the Lesbian Muses. In *On For Young and Old: Australian Intergenerational Radical Lesbian Feminist Anthology*, edited by Claudia Huber, Ardy Tibby, Barbary Clarke and Jean Taylor, Melbourne: Long Breast Press, pp. 174–189.

The Sacking of the Muses. 2017. NastyWomenAreEverywhere <http://www.nastywomeneverywhere.org/2017/02/the-sacking-of-the-muses/>

2017 Cyane. In *Metamorphic: 21st Century Poets Respond to Ovid,* edited by Nessa O'Mahony and Paul Munden. Canberra: Recent Work Press, pp. 73–74.

2014 Uṣas published under the title The Uṣasah. *Tincture Journal*, Issue 13, pp. 93–97.

2013 Uṣas published under the title The Uṣasah. *Lesbians Write On: A Celebration of Contemporary Australian Lesbian Writing*, edited by Anah Holland-Moore, Ardy Tibby, Barbary Clarke, Claudia Huber, Jean Taylor, and Rosalinda Rayne. Melbourne: Long Breast Press, pp 125–127.

2013 Trijaṭā's dream. *Poems 2013: Volume 2 of the Australian Poetry Ltd Members' Anthology*, edited by Jessica Friedmann, Denis Haskell and Chris Wallace-Crabbe, p. 97.

2012 Trijata's dream. *Island 130*, p. 133.

2012 Meghaḍūta: Twenty stanzas translated from Kalidasa's Sanskrit poem. *Mascara*. Issue 11, June: <http://mascarareview.com/susan-hawthorne-translates-kalidasas-meghaduta/>

2011 Pooja Rooms. *Inscribe: Northern Notes for Writers and Readers*. Issue Four, Winter, p. 11.

2010 Fragment 16. *Sinister Wisdom*. Fall 2010. Number 81, p. 7.

2009 Notes toward a Poem about Madhu / Honey Demon; Sarasvatikanthabharana: The Necklace of Sarasvati; *Sinister Wisdom*, Spring. Number 76, pp. 8–17.

2007 Sappho's butterfly, *Read These Lips.*

2007 Sense, *Sinister Wisdom.* Winter 2007–2008. Number 72, p. 48.

2007 Patriarchal grammar, *Sinister Wisdom.* Spring. Number 71, p. 19.

Thanks to my co-Sanskritists Greg Bailey, Christine Street, Rye Senjen and McComas Taylor who have kept me going through the syntactic and semantic jungles. Thanks to my cover endorsers: Robin Morgan, Donna Snyder and Suniti Namjoshi, and to all who have worked on this book: Helen Christie, Deb Snibson, Pauline Hopkins, Maralann Damiano, Rachael McDiarmid and Caitlin Roper. Undying thanks to my partner Renate Klein for multiple readings, and for love.

If you would like to know more about Spinifex Press,
write to us for a free catalogue, visit our website,
follow us on social media or email us for further information.

Spinifex Press
PO Box 105
Mission Beach QLD 4852
Australia

www.spinifexpress.com.au
women@spinifexpress.com.au